18 DAYS UNDERGROUND
AND OTHER INCREDIBLE RESCUE STORIES

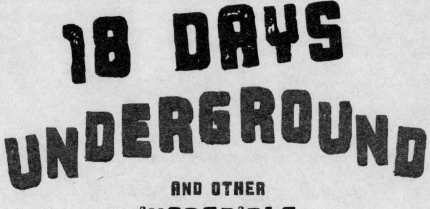

18 DAYS UNDERGROUND

AND OTHER INCREDIBLE RESCUE STORIES

BY JOANNE MATTERN

SCHOLASTIC INC.

ISBN 978-1-338-57175-2

10 9 8 7 6 5 4 3 2 1   19 20 21 22 23

Printed in the U.S.A.   40
First printing 2019

TABLE OF CONTENTS

THE RESCUED AND THE RESCUERS

Few people are surprised to hear about firefighters rushing into a burning building, or police officers protecting the public, or soldiers defending their comrades in battle.

But anyone can be a hero. There are many ordinary people who have taken part in dramatic rescues. A rescuer can be any age. He or she can live in any part of the world. All it takes is being in the right place at the right time and being willing to jump into action to help someone.

People in need of rescue need to be brave too. Imagine being trapped for weeks in an underground cave, or getting lost in a blizzard, or trying to escape a wildfire. It's easy to panic and lose hope in these kinds of situations. But many people in trouble show their bravery as they wait for help and even take steps to aid in their own escape.

In this book, you'll read the stories of more than ten dramatic rescues. Some of these rescues took place underground. Others happened in fires, blizzards, or hurricanes. In each story, you'll meet the real people who endured terrible situations as they waited to be rescued. And you'll meet their rescuers—everyone from a teenage boy and trained navy divers to a dog who had no special training but knew just what to do to help someone in need.

So get comfortable and dive into this collection of true stories that feature desperate situations, everyday heroes, and the courageous steps they took when help was needed the most.

18 DAYS UNDERGROUND

Rain was in the forecast on June 23, 2018. But the twelve young members of the Wild Boars soccer team and their coach weren't worried about the weather. Instead, they were ready to celebrate. That day was team member Peerapat Sompiangjai's seventeenth birthday. He and his teammates, plus their coach, Ekkapol "Ake" Chantawong, had their usual Saturday practice. Then they decided to set off on another adventure.

The teens and their coach rode their bikes up into the hills near their homes in the rural Mae Sai area of Thailand. Soon they reached the entrance to Tham Luang cave. Tham Luang was a favorite place for the boys to explore. They had been there many times and always had fun wiggling through the narrow corridors, climbing over rocks, and exploring for miles. Sometimes they even wrote new team members' names on the walls to welcome them.

But Tham Luang was a dangerous place. The cave system was completely cut off from the outside world. No GPS could navigate it, and no cell phone or Wi-Fi signals reached inside the rocky walls. Much of the cave system wasn't even on maps, and cave explorers (*spelunkers*) called it one of the most dangerous caves in the world.

The biggest danger in Tham Luang was water.

During the rainy season, torrents of water rush through the cave, flooding it for miles. Local officials even put a sign at the entrance to the cave warning people not to enter during the rainy season.

Peerapat and his friends weren't worried about any of this. They had explored the cave many times without any problems, and they didn't think today would be any different. So they dropped their bikes and backpacks at the entrance and raced inside carrying just their flashlights. They planned to stay for only an hour or so.

Then it began to rain.

A heavy downpour flooded into the cave, filling the passageways with rushing, muddy water. The flash flood surprised all of the Wild Boars. They had no choice but to venture deeper inside the cave to escape the deadly current. In no time at all, the boys and their coach were trapped, huddled on a twelve-foot ledge just above the water.

It didn't take long for the boys' families to wonder where they were. Someone saw that the team had discussed going into Tham Luang in a group chat the day before. Family members rushed to the cave. When they saw the bikes and bags at the entrance, they knew their worst fears were true. The boys were inside the cave. But where?

Local officials and rescue crews came to the cave, but there wasn't much they could do. The team could be anywhere inside the long, deep cave system. Were they even still alive? Or had they drowned in the rushing water?

While rescuers struggled to figure out what to do, the boys tried to make the best of their situation. They used rocks to dig out the soft limestone walls and make their shelf bigger. Then they waited in the darkness. The only sound was the rushing water.

Many people would panic in this situation. But the Wild Boars had a secret weapon—their coach, Ake Chantawong. Ake was only twenty-five years old, about ten years older than most members of his team. But he had once been a monk. Coach Ake used his spiritual training well. He led the boys in meditation. He told them to keep still to conserve their energy and their air supply. Most of all, he kept them calm in the overwhelming darkness.

Outside the cave, rescuers were hard at work. A team of Thai Navy SEALs joined the police and local volunteers to figure out where the boys were and how to get them out. Rescuers tried pumping out water. They drilled holes in the mountain. They even sent drones armed with heat sensors into the passageways in a desperate effort to find the boys.

Meanwhile, family members and neighbors waited outside the cave. They lit candles and prayed. "I want to show respect to the spirit that protects the cave," said Coach Ake's godmother, who also brought incense and fruit to offer the spirit. "I asked her to protect the thirteen kids," she explained.

Classmates of the Wild Boars did not forget about their trapped friends. They prayed together and posted messages on social media urging everyone not to give up hope. They even went to the cave and sang songs into the darkness in case the Wild Boars could hear them and understand that the world had not forgotten them. People from all over Thailand, and all over the world, came to help. All the while, rain continued to fall and the water in the cave grew higher.

Rescuers zeroed in on an area in the cave called Pattaya Beach. This underground place was a favorite spot for team gatherings and was usually dry, but this storm had flooded the beach as well. Maybe the boys were nearby.

Specially trained cave divers from Thailand, Great Britain, the United States, Australia, and other countries joined the rescue effort. Divers made many risky trips inside the cave. On one of these trips, they were excited to find an empty chamber. Although the boys weren't there, the divers could use the space, which they called Chamber Three, as a base for swimming deeper into the cave.

Finally, on July 2, more than a week after the Wild Boars disappeared, two British divers smelled something really bad. They shouted into the darkness. A few minutes later, they were greeted by an incredible sight. The Wild Boars were walking toward them, holding up their flashlights. The terrible smell was their body waste and sweat. "We smelled the children before we heard or saw them," diver John Volanthen recalled.

When John saw the first few boys coming toward them, he asked, "How many of you?"

"Thirteen!" the boys replied. John and his partner, Rick Stanton, couldn't believe it.

"They're all alive!" Rick said.

News that the boys had been found sent a wave of rejoicing through the rescuers and the families gathered outside the cave. John and Rick filmed the boys on their cameras and showed the video to the waiting crowds. The good news spread around the world. Meanwhile, divers sent food, air tanks, and other supplies in to the boys. For the Wild Boars, who had nothing to eat and had been licking water off the cave walls to survive, this was a wonderful gift. The boys were also happy that a military doctor and two Navy SEALs would stay with them in the cave and do their best to keep them safe.

The Wild Boars had been found, but they weren't saved yet. John and Rick and the other divers had faced incredibly difficult conditions just to get this far. The boys were more than a mile beneath the surface and more than two miles from the entrance. All the passageways that led inside were flooded. The water was muddy and cold, and the passages were dark and narrow.

There was no way the boys and their coach could swim out. In fact, some of the boys did not even know how to swim. Rescue seemed impossible. But the rescue teams refused to give up. "Now the real hard work comes," one diver told the media. If the boys could not swim out, maybe rescuers could swim in and get them. Rescuers began working on a new and daring plan.

Then, on July 6, tragedy struck. A former Thai Navy SEAL diver named Saman Gunan was on a routine run to deliver air tanks to the boys. For some reason, he ran out of air in his own tank and lost consciousness inside the cave. His dive buddy pulled him out and tried to save him, but it was too late. Saman was dead.

Saman's death hit everyone hard. Saman was fit and healthy. He had taken part in triathlons and was in top physical shape. Still, the cave had killed him. People wondered how the boys could ever come out alive if a trained navy diver couldn't survive.

Despite the tragedy, rescuers kept working. Time was running out. The air supply in the boys' cavern was getting lower every day. They had to get out soon.

Finally, rescuers came up with a way for the boys to swim out of the cave. But because the waters were dangerous for even experienced divers, the boys couldn't make the journey alone. Two divers would escort each boy through the flooded passageways.

Even this plan had many obstacles. Because the passageways were so narrow, the divers could not swim next to the boys. Instead, one diver would swim in front of a boy while the other diver swam behind. The boys would also need to wear oxygen masks and carry air tanks for the journey because much of the trip would be made underwater.

On Sunday, July 7—two weeks after the boys disappeared into Tham Luang—rescuers sprang into action. The rain had finally stopped, and the forecast was clear for the next few days. Everyone knew this break in the weather was the best chance of getting the Wild Boars out alive.

The journey would be divided into two parts. During the first part, divers would lead the boys from their rocky hideout to Chamber Three. This would be the most difficult part of the journey. Rescuers had to swim through pitch-black, freezing-cold waters and feel their way by holding on to a guide rope. Some sections were so narrow that the boys and their air tanks had to be lifted up and passed from one diver to the other. The boys would wear full face masks that pumped air into their lungs. They were also given medicine to keep them calm. Later, the media reported that the boys had, in fact, been given powerful drugs to make them sleep through the rescue. Their hands and arms were also tied down so they wouldn't panic and pull off the face masks.

The second part of the journey led from Chamber Three to the surface. For this part, the boys were strapped onto stretchers. In some places, the stretchers were passed from one rescuer to another. The stretchers were attached to a pulley that lifted them up a steep hill to the surface. Each part of the journey would take several hours.

Once they started, the rescues went surprisingly smoothly. One by one, the boys were brought out alive and rushed to waiting ambulances. Four boys were rescued the first day. Four more emerged on the second day.

But on the third day, as one of the last boys was being brought out, something went terribly wrong. As with the other rescues, the diver accompanying the boy tugged on the guide rope to signal rescuers at the surface that he was almost there. Fifteen minutes passed. Then an hour. Then another half hour went by with no sign of the diver and the boy. What had gone wrong? Where were the diver and his precious cargo?

Finally, the diver and the boy came out. It turned out that the diver had lost his hold on the rope and gotten disoriented. He was unable to find the way out. Instead, he backtracked to one of the rescues and got his bearings. Only then could he continue and find his way to the surface.

On day three, the last five boys and Coach Ake were brought to safety. Soon afterward, the doctor and the Navy SEALs who had stayed with the boys made their way out as well.

All of the boys and Coach Ake spent several days in the hospital. The boys were in surprisingly good spirits. They asked for their favorite foods, including fried chicken and fried rice, but doctors made them eat small amounts of plain foods at first so their bodies could get used to eating again. Finally, one by one, the boys went home.

People all over the world rejoiced at the amazing rescue. One diver said, "We are not sure if this is a miracle, science, or what." In the end, it didn't really matter. The boys and their coach were heroes, and so were the divers who rescued them. The world was united in hope and joy as the rescue unfolded. And everyone learned that miracles really can happen when people work together toward a common goal.

A FURRY FRIEND

melia Milling loved to hike. The twenty-one-year-old spent as much time as she could in the outdoors. Amelia was deaf, but she never let that get in the way of her sense of adventure or her love for the outdoors.

Amelia was from Tennessee, but in June 2018, she was far from home. Instead of being in the warm south, Amelia was on vacation in Alaska. She was thrilled to be hiking and exploring the rugged mountains and forests, which were so different from her southern home.

On that fateful June day, Amelia was hiking the Crow Pass Trail in Chugach State Park. The nearest city, Anchorage, was about thirty miles away. Earlier in the trip, Amelia had been with friends, but for this hike she was alone. Amelia wasn't worried, however. She was an experienced hiker, and she had a tent and other gear with her. She was sure she was ready for anything.

She wasn't.

Amelia was about four miles into her hike when disaster struck. Her *trekking poles*—long wooden poles that helped her keep her balance on the rough path—suddenly snapped. Amelia's feet slipped out from under her. The next thing she knew, she was tumbling down the hill.

The young woman fell about three hundred feet down the mountain through the snow. Her helpless body slammed into a boulder, sending her hurtling through the air and down another three hundred feet. "I felt like I was flying," she later described her out-of-control fall. Finally, Amelia came to rest in the snow. Amazingly, she wasn't hurt, other than some bruises and scrapes. But she was lost and alone.

Except she wasn't alone. A large white animal was running through the snow toward her. At first, Amelia thought it was a wolf, and her heart skipped a beat in fear. But as the animal came closer, Amelia saw it was a dog. The big white husky was wearing a collar and tag that read CROW CREEK GUIDE DOG. Later, Amelia found out the dog's name was Nanook, and he belonged to a man who lived near the trail.

The dog seemed eager to help, so Amelia decided to try hiking back to safety. Nanook led Amelia back to the trail, and the two hiked until it began to get dark. Then Amelia pitched her tent and crawled inside. She motioned for the dog to join her, but Nanook seemed happy to go to sleep just outside her tent.

The next morning, Amelia expected Nanook to be gone, but when she crawled out of her tent, he was there waiting for her. "When I opened up the tent, he was ready to go," Amelia marveled. "I realized he really was sticking with me when he greeted me in the morning when I unzipped my tent. He had stayed the entire night next to me."

The two continued their trek for hours. "He gave me the motivation to get up and walk another seven miles," Amelia later explained. "If he didn't show up, I probably wouldn't have gotten back up and kept walking that much."

After half a day's hike, Amelia and Nanook reached Eagle River. The fast-moving river was fed by a glacier, and the water was icy cold. Nanook seemed sure of a good place to cross and swam across to the other side. Amelia took a few minutes to rearrange the items in her pack so they would stay dry. By the time she was ready, the water looked rougher and faster than it had before. Amelia couldn't summon up the courage to step into the raging water.

Maybe there is a better place to cross, Amelia thought. She found another spot where the water looked calmer, but when she waded into the water, she lost her balance and fell into the rushing river. Within seconds, Amelia was soaked to the skin and freezing cold.

That's when Nanook leaped into action. The dog bounded into the water and grabbed the strap of Amelia's backpack in his teeth. Nanook pulled and Amelia pushed, and she was finally able to get across to the riverbank.

Amelia was dazed and so cold, she was afraid she might be going into shock. She changed into dry clothes and snuggled into her sleeping bag.

All she wanted was to warm up and go to sleep.

Nanook had other ideas. The dog began licking her. The licking was not "I want to play with you," Amelia later told her mother. "He just would not leave me alone." Amelia understood the dog wanted her to take action. The hiker realized that she might finally be close enough to civilization to summon help.

Before she left on her Alaskan adventure, her mother had insisted she bring a device called a SPOT beacon, which uses a GPS and satellite technology to find a person's location. Amelia hit the SOS button on the device, sending a signal that she hoped would alert rescuers. After she pushed the button, Nanook seemed calmer. Amelia huddled in her sleeping bag with the dog lying close beside her.

Amelia's signal reached the Alaska State Troopers. A few hours later, the thrum of a helicopter filled the air. Rescuers spotted Amelia in her bright red sleeping bag, Nanook still faithfully at her side.

Once Amelia and Nanook were safely in the helicopter, she shared her story with the state troopers. Trooper Eric Olsen was amazed to find out that Nanook had rescued Amelia and saved her life. He called the phone number of Nanook's tag and reached the owner, Scott Swift. Then, once Amelia was safely at the hospital, Olsen drove Nanook back home.

Scott Swift wasn't really surprised to find out his dog was a hero. It wasn't the first time Nanook had come to someone's rescue. "About two years ago, there was one other girl about six years old—he saved her when she fell in the river," Scott said. He explained that the dog is a "free spirit" who disappears for days at a time and often returns home with hikers or skiers who have befriended the dog on the trail.

Still, Scott was amazed to hear of his dog's latest rescue. "It sends chills up my spine when I think about it. I certainly didn't train him to do anything like this," he told news reporters. "It's a pretty powerful feeling that this dog had this instinctual ability to want to go help people."

The Alaska State Troopers agreed. Soon after the event, they named Nanook an Honorary State Trooper. Trooper Olsen said, "He's Alaska's version of Lassie."

As for Amelia Milling, she went back to her hiking trip after being checked out by doctors in an Anchorage hospital. And she made sure to spend some time with Nanook, her new best friend.

LOST AT SEA

Aldi Novel Adilang's job wasn't supposed to be dangerous. The worst thing about it was that Aldi spent hours alone with nothing to do, so things could get pretty boring. The eighteen-year-old lived on a fishing hut called a *rompong*. The rompong sat on a wooden platform and floated in the Pacific Ocean, more than seventy-five miles away from his home in Indonesia. Aldi's main job was to light lamps on the hut at night to attract fish into traps underneath the platform.

Aldi was supposed to live in the hut for six months. Once a week, a ship brought supplies to him. Otherwise, he was alone in the middle of the ocean. But soon he would be more alone than he ever could have dreamed.

On the morning of July 14, 2018, high winds battered the hut. Aldi stayed safely inside under the protection of the hut's thatched roof during the storm. The rompong had been through storms before, so the teenager wasn't too worried that anything would happen. He was wrong.

About seven o'clock that morning, Aldi felt a sharp tug on the bottom of the rompong. A sudden gust of wind had snapped the rope that anchored the hut to the seafloor. Suddenly, the rompong was moving. Aldi was helpless to stop the hut as it floated away on the rising ocean waves.

In time, the storm passed and the winds

died down. But Aldi was in big trouble. Far from land and with no ships in sight, he was alone in the middle of nowhere. Aldi grabbed a radio he kept in the hut in case of trouble. He called his friends who were working on other rompongs. "Phone the boss," he told them. "My anchor has snapped." But there was no answer. Maybe he was too far out to sea for anyone to pick up the signal.

At first, Aldi wasn't too worried. The same thing actually had happened to him twice before. Each time, people from the company he worked for had found him in a few days. "On the first day I was okay," Aldi said later. "I wasn't stressed or panicking. I knew they would send a boat, but I was worried it would have to turn back because the winds and the waves were strong."

Meanwhile, Aldi tried to look on the bright side. He had shelter, food, water, and cooking gas. He was sure someone would come looking for him soon. To pass the time, Aldi sang songs, made a calendar to mark off the days, and read the Bible. And he kept looking for boats on the horizon.

But as the days passed, Aldi began to get scared. His supply of food was soon gone, even though he rationed it to last as long as possible. He caught fish from the ocean and cooked them on the small stove in the hut.

Running out of water was a bigger problem. Aldi's supply of fresh water was used up. Rainstorms provided some fresh water for him. But without rain, Aldi had no fresh water. It was cruel to look out over the ocean and see nothing but water he couldn't drink. Aldi knew drinking the salty ocean water would make him sick and could even kill him. But he had to think of something.

Then Aldi got an idea. Maybe he could strain

the salt out of the ocean water. Aldi pulled up his T-shirt, which had gotten wet from the sea. He squeezed out a few drops of water and sucked them into his mouth. The water wasn't too salty! Aldi had found a way to make fresh water out of salt water. The small victory cheered him up.

But the teenager soon faced another problem. He was out of cooking gas. How could he cook his food? Aldi did the only thing he could think of. He burned the rompong's wooden fences to build a fire. Once again, Aldi's cleverness saved the day and made him feel hopeful.

More days passed, then weeks. Aldi didn't know what to think. Surely people were looking for him? He thought about his family. Did they miss him? Did they wonder what had happened to him? Maybe everyone thought he had drowned and had called off the search? "The hardest thing was the thought that I would never see my parents again," he said. "That I would never see my island again, and never make it home alive." Aldi tried not to think these dark thoughts, but it was hard not to panic as time went on and on. Alone on his floating hut, he cried tears of sadness and fear.

The ocean waves carried Aldi farther east every day. Soon the young man had no idea where he was. There was nothing to see but water in every direction. Then, one day, Aldi saw a ship on the horizon. His hopes soared! Surely he would be rescued!

Aldi jumped up and down on the deck of the rompong. He waved his arms and yelled. Then he realized the awful truth. The huge ship was too far away to see him. Desperate to make contact, Aldi grabbed his radio and tried to make contact with the ship. To his delight, the captain answered. He promised to come back and get Aldi after the crew finished their day's work. Aldi was thrilled. But hours passed with no sign of the ship returning. Aldi realized they weren't coming back. He was still alone.

"Another ship will come," Aldi told himself. "Surely the next ship will see me." Aldi was right—another ship did come past. In fact, more than ten ships came in sight. Each time, Aldi tried to call them on his radio while he waved frantically for help. Each time the huge freighters and tankers sailed right by him. The teenager knew he was nothing but a speck on the ocean to them. Even if they sailed right by, they couldn't see him, floating alone in the vast ocean.

It was August 31. Aldi had been at sea for forty-eight days. He had run out of wood to burn, so he had no way to cook the fish he caught. Aldi had no choice but to eat them raw.

Aldi didn't know it, but the ocean currents had carried him hundreds of miles until he was near the island of Guam. And his bad luck was finally about to change.

Once again, Aldi saw a ship sailing toward him. It was a cargo ship from Panama, halfway around the world, called the MV *Arpeggio*. As he had so many times before, Aldi turned on his radio. This time, he was able to find the same frequency the *Arpeggio* was using. "Help, help, help!" Aldi called. He stood on the deck and waved a towel at the ship, which seemed so far away. Would anyone even hear or see him?

Suddenly, a voice spoke back to him. It was the ship's chief mate, Emmanuel Soriano. Aldi didn't understand the words Soriano said to him, but his heart leaped with hope. Someone knew he was alive!

On board the *Arpeggio*, Soriano hurried to find the ship's captain, Narciso Santillan. He told Santillan about the distress call and the tiny hut floating at sea. Immediately,

Santillan ordered the huge ship to change course. The cargo ship was about to become a rescue ship.

Aldi rejoiced as he saw the ship coming closer and closer. But then he got scared. The ship was so big, and his rompong was so tiny. What if the *Arpeggio* hit him by accident? Or what if it could not send any help down to the small raft? Would Aldi be lost at sea once again? All he could do was hold his breath, hope, and pray.

Aldi was right to worry. The giant cargo ship couldn't just pull up to the rompong. At first, it couldn't even get close enough to Aldi to res-cue him. It took four tries before the *Arpeggio* could come near the rompong without creating huge waves that could have swamped the hut.

Finally, Captain Santillan moved his ship as close as he could. Crew members threw a life preserver into the water. Aldi grabbed it and kicked his way through the water to the side of the cargo ship. But his ordeal wasn't over yet.

Crew members lowered a wooden ladder over the side of the ship. Aldi managed to grab hold of the bottom rungs. Then he began a terrifying climb up the side of the huge ship, the ladder twisting and turning under his weight.

A few times, Aldi got stuck between the ladder and the side of the ship. He had to stop and rest many times. At last, he climbed his way close enough to the top. Crew members grabbed him and pulled him to safety.

For a few minutes, Aldi did not have the strength to do anything besides sit on the deck and catch his breath. Crew members wrapped him in a blanket and gave him water to drink. Someone brought him a plate full of bread.

Crew members tried to speak to Aldi, but they could not understand one another's language.

They had to communicate through gestures and hand signals. Amazingly, after about five minutes, Aldi stood up. He shook hands with a crew member and smiled. Someone pulled up Google Translate on a computer. Using that technology, Aldi was able to tell his story to the astonished crew.

Aldi's journey was not over yet, however. Captain Santillan spoke to officials over the radio. His new passenger had no passport, no identification, nothing but the clothes on his back. Because the cargo ship had been headed to Japan, officials told Santillan to continue to that country. Aldi's paperwork would be taken care of when he arrived.

On September 6, Aldi and his new friends arrived in Japan. From there he traveled to Tokyo, where he got on an airplane. Soon afterward, he landed in Indonesia. Aldi was finally home.

On September 9, Aldi was reunited with his family. Aldi was thrilled to be back home and to see his relatives. And he made all of them and himself a promise. From now on, he was staying on dry land!

A RESCUER GETS
RESCUED

r. Stephen Kimmel looked nervously out of his window. It was August 26, 2017, and Kimmel's home, along with all of the Houston, Texas, area was being pounded by Hurricane Harvey. Sheets of rain poured down outside, whipped by high winds. The storm was terrifying, and it was not going away anytime soon.

Dr. Kimmel was happy to be safe inside the

house with his family. Then, about ten o'clock that night, the phone rang. It was a doctor from Clear Lake Regional Medical Center, where Dr. Kimmel was a surgeon who treated children. The caller had disturbing news. A teenage boy named Jacob had suffered a serious injury. If someone could perform surgery to fix the damage within the next six hours, the boy would be okay. If not, he would be left with permanent damage. No other surgeons were available. Could Dr. Kimmel get from his house to Clear Lake Regional Medical Center to perform the surgery?

Dr. Kimmel didn't have to think twice. He promised to get to the hospital as soon as he could. Then he set out into the storm.

The rain was pouring down harder than Dr. Kimmel had ever seen, but he started his car and carefully drove out to the road. He hadn't gone far when he had to stop. Instead of the road in front of him, there was a huge lake of water. Dr. Kimmel knew that if he drove into the water, his car would stall. Even more dangerous, he could be swept away. Dr. Kimmel had no choice but to turn around and go back home.

However, the doctor wasn't about to give up. He called the hospital and explained the problem to the chief medical officer. The medical officer called Dr. Kimmel's local fire department.

About one thirty in the morning, two soaking-wet firefighters, Kevin Mikulan and his friend Zeke, arrived at Kimmel's door. "Where's your truck?" Dr. Kimmel asked.

"The water's too high here," the firefighters responded. "We're going to run for a while." The three men ran through the water, which was rising higher by the minute. After sloshing through the flood for about a mile, they finally reached the truck. Dr. Kimmel was surprised to see a canoe on board. "I thought we were going to get into a big shiny truck, and we were just going to drive out," the doctor said. That's not exactly what happened.

The firefighters and Dr. Kimmel set off in the truck. For a while, they were able to make it through the rising water, but they soon reached an area where the road was washed out altogether. Dr. Kimmel realized it was time to use the canoe.

The doctor and the two firemen squeezed into the canoe and started paddling. It was a dangerous journey. As they paddled down a major highway, cars passed them on the left and right. "We had to be careful not to get hit," Kimmel said.

Along the way, they passed people stranded on top of the roofs of their half-submerged cars. Dr. Kimmel realized they needed help more than he did. "You take the boat and help those people," he told the firefighters. "I can make it from here."

It was another mile to the hospital. Dr. Kimmel waded through waist-deep water, barely able to see through the blinding rain. It was after two thirty in the morning when he finally reached the hospital. The drenched doctor changed into surgical scrubs and went straight to the operating room to work on his patient. To everyone's relief, the surgery was a complete success.

"Sometimes you have to do whatever it takes," Dr. Kimmel reflected. "This young man's life would have been changed for the worse forever if we hadn't been able to perform surgery when we did. In the end, it all turned out very well."

Jacob Terrazas, the teen who was waiting for surgery, had his own frightening rescue story to tell. After his injury, a paramedic started driving him to the hospital in his truck, but the floodwaters soon became too high to drive through.

"I was really scared," Jacob told reporters after his ordeal. "We had to get out of the truck. One of the paramedics carried me to the side of the highway and after that we waited. I was getting wet, cold. We were all cold."

Jacob, his family, and the paramedics waited in the rain for a fire truck to reach them. When the teen finally arrived at the hospital, he didn't even realize Kimmel was his doctor because the older man had just arrived there himself and wasn't in medical attire.

"It was kind of weird because I got there, and I didn't know who the doctor was because he was just like some dude," Jacob said. "That's what my mom thought, too."

Dr. Kimmel's long night of rescues wasn't over, however. After he finished the surgery,

Dr. Kimmel called home to check on his wife and children. The news was not good. His wife told him their house was flooding. There was five feet of water inside the home. She and the children were trapped on the second floor as the water rose higher. The doctor realized it was time for another rescue.

A quick call to the Coast Guard and help was on the way. A boat picked up the doctor's family and brought them to the hospital. The family spent the night sleeping on the floor of Dr. Kimmel's office, but they were happy to be safe, dry, and together.

A year after his dramatic night in the water, Dr. Kimmel and his firefighter rescuers were honored by the hospital. "You touched a young man's life . . . and I want to thank you for that," Todd Caliva, Clear Lake Regional Medical Center's CEO, told Dr. Kimmel as he presented him with the award. "You're our hero. You're my hero. I know you're that family's hero."

Dr. Kimmel knew he wasn't the only hero that night. He would never forget the firefighters and Coast Guard personnel who helped so many people during that wet and windy storm.

A BUS RIDE THROUGH FIRE

Kevin McKay was worried. He had been a bus driver for only a few months, and normally his job driving children to and from Ponderosa Elementary School in Paradise, California, was not that exciting. But today was different. Today, Paradise was on fire. And it was up to McKay to get a bus full of children to safety.

The wildfire started on November 8, 2018.

Called the Camp Fire, it was one of several major wildfires that devastated parts of Northern California. Flames roared through woods and into neighborhoods. Houses, stores, and other buildings had no chance against the fire, which consumed everything in its path. Even schools weren't safe from the flames.

McKay had seen wildfires before, but this one really scared him. He had never seen a fire where flames came down from so many different directions. His family had evacuated the area a few days earlier, but McKay stayed behind to concentrate on his job. "I just knew that things were going to continue to escalate," he said.

Many of the children at Ponderosa Elementary had also evacuated. But that morning, as the fire grew closer, almost two dozen children were still at the school. The school principal decided that the children had to get out of there. McKay, who happened to be at the school with an empty bus, said he was up to the job.

Around eight o'clock that morning, twenty-two children walked through the smoky air and climbed onto the bus. Two teachers, Abbie Davis and Mary Ludwig, climbed on board as well. The school principal followed behind them in his truck.

McKay started down the road, but it was slow going. By nine o'clock, an hour into the journey, they had only gone a few blocks. Everyone was trying to get out of town, and the road was packed with cars.

McKay inched along, barely able to move the bus through the heavy traffic. He and the teachers wondered if they should abandon the bus. But they knew they didn't have a chance of getting out on foot. So McKay drove on.

Meanwhile, Ludwig and Davis walked up

and down the aisle of the bus. They asked older children to buddy up with younger ones. The teachers spoke to the children and kept them calm.

Keeping calm became harder to do as the bus began to fill with smoke. McKay was impressed with both the teachers and the students, whom he called "little troupers." But the children were scared and so were the teachers. "The sky was really menacing," Ludwig later said. "It was very scary. It looked like Armageddon."

An hour later, the bus had traveled only about two miles. "It was dark and smoky and beginning to get more and more dark, almost like dusk," McKay said. The children got even more nervous. As the bus inched past a burning McDonald's restaurant and other burning buildings, the children started to panic.

"I can't breathe!" one child cried. Others said they felt sleepy or sick from the smoke. McKay knew he had to act fast to keep his young passengers safe. But what could he do?

Just then, a young man approached the bus and held up a water bottle. McKay opened the door, and the man handed the bottle to him. He explained that he knew there were children on the bus and wanted to help, but he had nothing to offer but the water bottle. The young man didn't know it, but his simple gift was just what the children on the bus needed.

McKay took off his shirt and poured the water bottle over it. The teachers tore the shirt into strips and gave one to each child to put over his or her mouth. The wet cloth helped filter the smoke and made it easier to breathe.

Ten-year-old Charlotte Merz was one of the students on the bus. She was scared but tried to think good thoughts and go to her "happy place." She later described the journey. "The smoke made it hard to see. It was so crazy, and there were fires left and right everywhere you looked," she said.

Suddenly, there was a huge bang on the side of the bus. It felt like someone had punched the vehicle. A car had hit the bus as it moved through the heavy traffic. McKay didn't stop to check. He drove on.

Then McKay saw someone waving for help on the side of the road. A preschool teacher from another school was stranded next to her broken-down car. McKay eased the bus over and opened the door. The teacher hurried on board and the journey continued.

As minutes stretched into hours, Abbie Davis wondered if she was going to die. The fire was everywhere, and the smoke was almost too thick to see through. She and the others said prayers. Davis knew she had to keep her own fear under control. "I held back from crying the entire time. But we were so focused on those kids, and that great responsibility is what really kept us focused," Davis said.

Finally, at two thirty, more than five hours after the fiery journey started, McKay made it to Biggs Elementary School, thirty miles away, where the families of the children and teachers were waiting anxiously. A relieved McKay delivered all of his passengers to safety and waited there until every child had been picked up. When Abbie Davis's husband arrived, he hugged McKay so hard, he almost lifted the bus driver off his feet.

McKay didn't see his family until later that night, and he lost his own home to the Camp Fire. The driver did not get excited over his daring rescue, but other people did. "I was where I was supposed to be," he said. "I feel blessed."

Mary Ludwig had a different explanation for their amazing and successful rescue. "We had the bus driver from heaven," she said.

THE 33

Imagine going to work every day in a mine miles underground. As you work, you sense the total darkness lurking just beyond the lights of your work area. You feel the tremendous presence of the mountain pressing down on you. You try not to think of what would happen if the mine caved in and trapped you in a tiny space deep under the surface of the Earth. That nightmare became all too real for a group of thirty-three miners in Chile.

On August 5, 2010, miners were hard at work in the San José Mine in Chile's Atacama Desert. Some work crews drilled for copper, gold, and other precious minerals. Others filled up dump trucks with minerals and drove them up a long ramp and out of the mine. A few men were on their break, resting in a cave-like chamber called the Refuge, where fresh air was pumped in from outside to relieve the terrible heat inside the mine.

Around one o'clock in the afternoon, Franklin Lobos and Jorge Galleguillos were driving a dump truck full of minerals down one of the winding roads inside the mine. They were about two thousand feet below the surface when they felt a strange vibration. Suddenly, a massive explosion rocked the mountain, sending thick clouds of dust down the passageway. Rocks tumbled around the men as they jumped out of the truck and rushed for safety. Lobos and Galleguillos were joined by other men, all running for their lives. They headed for the safety of the Refuge.

As the dust settled, the men realized what had happened. A huge slab of rock, as tall as a forty-five-story building and weighing more than 700,000 tons, had broken off from the mountain and crashed down into the mine. That crash set off a chain reaction of more falling rocks as the mountain caved in on itself.

Luis Urzua, the shift supervisor, knew there were men trapped in the tunnels beneath him. He and a few other miners made their way down the dusty, rock-strewn passageways and rounded up as many men as they could find. Urzua led them back to the Refuge. Then he counted heads. There were thirty-three men there, ranging in age from eighteen to sixty-three.

Even worse, the men discovered that the

air pumps, electricity, and the communication system in the Refuge had all been cut off by the falling rocks. The men were alone with only the weak lights of their headlamps to light the stone space.

Several groups of men tried to reach the opening to the mine. They climbed and wiggled up different air shafts and looked for emergency ladders mounted into the walls. But every attempt ended in failure. The stone that crashed down blocked every possible route to the surface. The men were trapped inside a stone tomb.

At the surface, news of the explosion sent other mine workers into action. Rescuers arrived quickly, but there was no way for them to get past the stone slab and into the mine. Everyone wondered if any workers were alive inside. Had they been killed by the explosion

and the rock fall? Or were they waiting some-
where under the ground, hoping for rescue?

Soon, government officials were on the
scene. They sent probes into the mine down
some of the shafts that were still open. Time
after time, the probes saw and heard nothing.

Meanwhile, the miners' families gathered
at the opening to the mine. They waited for
news, hoping and praying that their husbands,
fathers, sons, and brothers were still alive.
When answers didn't come quickly enough,
they banged drums and shouted at the police
guarding the entrance to the mine. But all anyone could do was wait.

Meanwhile, the miners tried to make the
best of their tiny prison. Shift supervisor Urzua
urged the men to work together. Each man was
given a job to do. On the first day, Urzua took
off the white helmet that marked him as the

supervisor. "We are all equal now," he told the others. "There are no bosses and employees."

One of the biggest problems the miners faced was food. They had only a small supply with them. The men agreed to ration what they had. Each man ate only a small spoonful of canned tuna and two cookies a day. They drank water that they drained from industrial tanks in the mine.

At last, on August 22, rescuers pulled up yet another probe. This time, there was great news. The probe had reached the Refuge and the trapped miners. One of the miners wrote a note and attached it to the probe. The note read, "We are fine in the shelter, the 33 of us."

At the surface, the crowds rejoiced at the news. But it was much too early to celebrate. Now that they knew the miners were alive, there was even more urgency to free them.

Finally, engineers came up with a difficult

but clever plan. They would drill another shaft into the mine. Then they would lower a rescue capsule down that shaft and lift the trapped miners out. That was the good news. The bad news was that the rock was so thick and the miners so deep, it would take weeks to reach them. Three drills began working around the clock to dig a tunnel through the mountain.

Workers tried to make the miners as comfortable as they could during the long weeks of work to free them. They sent down food and cameras. The miners made videos of themselves and sent them back up to the surface so their families could see them. The miners said they were all healthy and in good spirits.

On October 9, the drill finally broke through to the Refuge. There were still a few more days of work to make the tunnel wide enough and prepare the rescue capsule. Then, just after midnight on October 13, as millions of people watched live on television, the first miner was pulled out of the mountain. More than twenty-two hours later, Luis Urzua was the last man freed. After sixty-nine days, the breathtaking rescue was finally over, with every one of the thirty-three miners safe and sound.

The mine rescue was an amazing and wonderful thing, but for the miners, their ordeal didn't end once they emerged into the desert sun. Many of them suffered from post-traumatic stress after the incident. They also struggled with becoming celebrities and the tremendous amount of attention they received from around the world. Still, all of the men and their families were grateful for their new chance at life after spending sixty-nine long, dark days underground.

LOST IN A BLIZZARD

Winters in the northern Canadian territory of Nunavut are cold and snowy, but the fierce conditions are a normal way of life for the people who live there. Still, even people who have lived in the area their whole lives can be taken by surprise and need rescuing. That's exactly what happened to twenty-two-year-old Paul Qulitalik Sr. and his thirteen-year-old cousin Mark.

On a cold Sunday night in November 2017, Paul and Mark set out from Mark's home in the town of Igloolik to travel to Paul's home in Hall Beach. Hall Beach was less than forty-five miles away, and the trip should have taken just a couple of hours by snowmobile. But the Qulitaliks never arrived. Their families reported them missing, but their ordeal was just beginning.

An unexpected blizzard had struck the travelers. High winds and heavy snow created whiteout conditions. Paul could no longer see the trail, and the travelers got lost. Paul decided that conditions were too dangerous to keep on going. They huddled together for warmth and tried to shelter from the drifting snow.

Paul was angry at himself for not bringing a *qamutik,* a sled that could be towed behind the snowmobile. Residents often used qamutiks to carry supplies, and that certainly would have come in handy on this cold, snowy night.

Instead, he and Mark had only their clothes and parkas and a couple of flashlights.

After a long night during which temperatures dropped to almost ten degrees below zero, Paul and Mark decided to continue their trip in the light of the next morning. But the blizzard was still roaring. Then things got worse—their snowmobile ran out of gas. There was nothing to do but wait.

Paul and Mark didn't have any tools, so they used their feet to stomp out a shelter next to the snowmobile. Then they huddled inside and tried to stay warm. The two often heard airplanes flying overhead. Mark tried to signal them with his flashlight, but it was impossible to see the light through the snow.

"Let's try to walk to Hall Beach," Paul decided after another cold night in the snow. The two set off on foot, but they didn't get far. The blizzard was still raging, and the snow, cold, and biting winds were too much. "We're safer back at the shelter," Paul decided. And so the two turned back.

Four long days passed. The stranded travelers had nothing to eat or drink. Would they ever be rescued? Or would they die together in the bitter cold and heavy snow?

Late Thursday night, the two decided to make another try at walking to Hall Beach. This time, they got as close as a few miles from their home community. Suddenly, they heard voices. To their relief, a group of rescuers came out of the snow.

"We saw your flashlight and decided to investigate," the rescue party said, pointing to Mark's flashlight, which he'd been using to light their steps. "Let's get you two inside."

Despite their ordeal, both Paul and Mark were in good health. Paul had a small area of frostbite on his thumb, but Mark had no injuries at all. "Thank God we were found alive and okay," Mark said happily. "Now we are in a warm place."

It wasn't long before Paul and Mark were back with their families. The whole community rejoiced with them. Igloolik mayor Celestino Uyarak said, "Everyone is waking up to this good news." Uyarak explained that many people in the community cried when they heard the reports of Paul and Mark's rescue. For their part, Paul and Mark were happy to be home.

Paul and Mark Qulitalik weren't the first Nunavut residents to need rescuing after being lost in a blizzard. More than a year earlier, Pauloosie Keyootak, a sixty-two-year-old member of Nunavut's legislature, had a similar adventure. In March 2016, Keyootak, along with his son, Atamie, and his nephew, Peter, set out on a 186-mile journey from the village of Iqaluit up the coast of Baffin Island. The trip should have taken between eleven and fifteen hours. The men had two snowmobiles and a qamutik sled carrying extra fuel and supplies. They also knew there were cabins to shelter in along the way. What could go wrong?

As it turned out, a lot. When a blizzard struck, the travelers got lost in the blowing, drifting snow. Instead of heading northeast, they got turned around and headed south instead. By the time they realized their mistake, they didn't have enough gas to go back. Keyootak decided the best thing to do was dig a shelter and wait for help.

Keyootak used his knife to dig out a small shelter. Meanwhile, Atamie and Peter shot a caribou. "That's how we survived—eating the meat from the caribou," Keyootak explained. The group also had a small camp stove, some fuel, tea and sugar, a sleeping bag, and a mat.

During the day, the men stayed outside,

looking for rescuers and moving around to keep warm. As soon as the sun went down, they huddled inside the shelter and slept. Days passed with no sign of help.

Meanwhile, Keyootak's family had reported the group missing. Search-and-rescue teams jumped into action. They had no doubt they would find the missing men. "We were pretty sure they'd be alive," said Ed Zebedee, a member of the team. "It was just a matter of finding them. You just keep plugging away."

Fortunately, the weather had cleared, and conditions were good for searching. With no snow or high winds, rescuers could use helicopters and planes to search the area. Other teams searched on the ground. Team members relied on tribal elders for help. "They know everything there is to know about the land," Zebedee said with admiration.

Finally, eight days after Keyootak and the

others had disappeared, rescuers in an airplane saw snowmobile tracks in the snow down below. They followed them and spotted the stranded snowmobilers' makeshift camp.

When the plane touched down, Keyootak was happier than he had ever been. He later told reporters he was crying for joy and "jumping happy." The three men were flown to a hospital, where everyone was checked out and found to be healthy.

Ed Zebedee was equally thrilled to see the men brought out safely. "I've been doing this work in Nunavut for thirty-six years," he said the day after the rescue. "A search like yesterday, I can stay a few more years."

TRAPPED IN THE TREES

The workers at Wild Florida, an animal park in central Florida, spend most of their days piloting airboats through the Everglades, taking tourists on rides to see alligators, birds, and other wildlife that live in the swamp. But the workers have another job, one that they only take on during hurricanes. When a bad storm strikes, the Wild Florida workers turn into rescuers. But none of them had ever been involved in a rescue as dramatic as the one they found themselves in after 2018's Hurricane Florence.

The powerful hurricane struck the southeastern part of the United States in September 2018. Floodwaters raged from Florida up to the Carolinas. The Wild Florida team jumped into action. With streets flooded from the heavy rain, the park's airboats were the perfect way to get around and find people trapped by the high waters.

Jordan Munns, PJ Brown, Sam Haught, and Daniel Munns loaded their airboats on a trailer and traveled north to Kelly, North Carolina. While they were patrolling the flooded streets, the team got a call that there was a family trapped in some fallen trees in the middle of the water. Jordan piloted one of the boats to the area. The water was rushing fast over the highway, with rapids sending other vehicles across the road in front of them. When Jordan and the others got there, they couldn't believe what they saw.

Kelli Massey and her family had driven to Florida to escape the hurricane and came back to their home in North Carolina too early. Their car got caught in a flash flood in North Carolina, and the family, including Kelli, her husband, their four-year-old daughter, eight-year-old son, an uncle, and a dog, were swept into the water. To make matters worse, Kelli was eight months pregnant.

The family managed to swim toward some fallen trees. They grabbed the branches and held on for their lives. It was hours before a rescue team tried to reach them, but the branches and debris were too thick for them to get close. The rescuers had to give up. Once again, Kelli and her family were alone in the raging water, scattered through the tangle of branches and trees.

After three hours in the dark, clinging to branches and pummeled by the cold, fast-moving water, Kelli's family was almost ready to give up. Kelli's four-year-old daughter was crying and saying she wanted to go home. Kelli told her, "We've just got to hold on." Kelli later remembered, "I wasn't thinking about any-thing but holding on to that branch."

After three hours in the water, the family heard the Wild Florida airboat approaching. Jordan kept switching the motor of the boat on and off so he could hear the family's cries and pinpoint where they were. Getting close enough was difficult work. "We were nudging from tree to tree in a very, very dense forest, that's ten to fifteen feet deep of water," Jordan said.

Finally, Jordan and his crew got close enough to see the family. The first person they saw was Kelli's husband, with their son on his back. After pulling them into the boat, the team continued into the trees until they saw Kelli with the four-year-old girl clinging to her back. Finally, the Wild Florida team rescued the family's uncle and their dog. The whole rescue took about thirty-five minutes.

"It was a reunion that they didn't think was going to happen," Jordan told the media after the rescue. Once the family was on the boat, they told their rescuers that they thought they were going to die. "A professional swift-water team couldn't get to them, they just thought and just came to grips with the fact that they were never going to see each other again, and they were going to die."

Not only did Kelli and her family not die, they were all released from a local hospital after a checkup. Kelli was worried that the stress of the ordeal might cause her baby to be born early, but the baby was fine and not in any danger.

The Wild Florida team stayed in the area throughout the weekend rescuing others and helping in any way they could. But they will never forget Kelli Massey and her family's ordeal. "It was pretty emotional. That's all I can say," Daniel Munns admitted through tears, still shaken by what he saw. "I had to sit in the truck because I was overwhelmed."

THE GOOD
NEIGHBOR

It was the end of a long day in September 2012, and fourteen-year-old Marcos Ugarte was doing homework. The Troutdale, Oregon, teen's father, Eduardo, was also home and helping Marcos with his work. That's when they heard screaming. The voices were coming from a house four doors away.

At first, Eduardo didn't think much of the noise. "I assumed they were just arguing," he said.

"I said to Marcos, 'Let's just leave them alone.'"

But Marcos wasn't satisfied. In addition to hearing the screaming, he had noticed something even more ominous. There was an orange glow coming from the house down the street. He realized what was happening was no family argument—their neighbor's house was on fire!

The high-school freshman and his father took off running. The burning house belonged to Alex Ma and his family, which included his wife, mother, and two young children. Marcos and his father barely knew the family and had never exchanged more than a smile and a quick hello with them. But that didn't matter now.

When Marcos and Eduardo arrived at the house, they saw a terrible sight. Alex Ma stumbled down the stairs after a failed attempt to rescue his seven-year-old son, Cody. "He had been completely engulfed in flames," Marcos said. "He had soot coming out of his nose and mouth; he had just ingested so much of it."

"I'll go in," Marcos said, but his father told him to wait. Then Eduardo ran into the house and crawled to the room where the neighbor's son was trapped. He crawled across the floor and touched the door, but it would not open. Cody had gotten so scared when he saw the fire, he ran into a bedroom and locked the door.

The smoke was so thick that Eduardo couldn't even stand up. Defeated, he went back outside. But the rescue was far from over.

Cody's grandmother was struggling to bring a ladder from the backyard. Marcos grabbed the ladder away from her and used it to climb to the second floor, where Cody was trapped. "My instincts took over. I saw the grandmother crying. I felt so bad for them, and I just wanted to help," he explained.

Marcos crawled up to the window and punched out the screen. Then he climbed inside, quickly scooped up the boy, and carried him to safety while his father held the ladder. "I knew I couldn't mess up because there was a life on the line," Marcos said.

When his father saw Marcos climbing into the burning house, he could hardly believe what was happening. But he wasn't really surprised at his son's actions. "There was just so much adrenaline going on," he said. "This doesn't surprise me that he just takes initiative and gets the job done. He is in my eyes a true hero."

Cody inhaled some smoke and was sent to the hospital to be checked out, but he was just fine. No one else was injured.

Marcos's father said giving a helping hand is second nature for Marcos, and showing kindness is something he does all the time. Marcos's two siblings suffer from a chronic illness, and he is always willing to help care for them. "I think it's awesome," the proud papa said.

"We've taught all of our kids to do what's right in the face of adversity. That doesn't mean we expect them to climb ladders into homes that are on fire, but if they see a problem, we expect them to do what they can to help."

Others thought Marcos's actions were pretty amazing too. Six months later, Marcos was honored with the Citizen Service Before Self Award. He and his family traveled to Washington, D.C., to accept the award from the Congressional Medal of Honor Society. This award is given to ordinary Americans who perform acts of courage and self-sacrifice that symbolize the American spirit. Marcos was the youngest person to ever receive the award.

Despite all the honors and attention, Marcos shrugged off his heroics. "I can't say I really consider myself a hero," he said. "I think anyone would have done what I did."

THE STRENGTH OF A TEAM

The Boise Black Knights had a good reason to celebrate. The youth football team had traveled to San Jose, California, from their home in Idaho to play in the Bay Area Spring Football Tournament of Champions in May 2018. The Black Knights had won the tournament. They thought the victory would be the most exciting moment of their trip, but an even more dramatic event was in store.

About eight thirty that night, the Black Knights' caravan was in the middle of the long road trip home. The players, tired and bored on the long ride, watched videos or played games to pass the time. But as they drove through southeastern Oregon, the red car driving in front of them suddenly went off the road and flipped over.

Coach Rudy Jackson remembered the moment: "We were all driving, they came around a corner and seen an accident with a car rolled over." They later found out that high winds had caused the car, carrying Alan and Margaret Hardman, to veer off the road and flip.

The team vans quickly pulled over. Coach Jackson and his players poured out of the vehicles to see if they could help the Hardmans, both of whom were trapped in their car. Working together, the boys pulled the trapped man out of his car. Then they went around to the other side to check on his wife.

The boys quickly realized that it would be impossible to free Margaret Hardman by pulling her out of the wreckage. The woman's seat belt was still on, so some of the team cut her free. At the same time, in an amazing show of strength and teamwork, a group of players grabbed the side of the car and lifted it up enough for Margaret to escape.

Teenager Regan Magill recorded the incident. "It wasn't really something we thought about," he said. "We just pulled over. I don't want to imagine what would happen if we were not there to help."

The team waited until ambulances arrived before getting back in their vans and heading on their way. When local police arrived, the team was gone and the officers had no idea about their livesaving help. It wasn't until local residents told them about the incident and police saw the video on social media that they realized what had happened.

The boys were praised for their quick, life-saving actions. "It's nice to see kids doing a good deed like this; I suspect they have some great coaches leading them," local under-sheriff Travis Johnson said. "It's hard to know exactly what would have happened if this team hadn't been there to rescue the trapped female, but as it is, it looks like everyone is going to be just fine."

The players were quick to praise their coach as well. "He taught us to play selfless football and not selfish—just help others out before yourself," Regan Magill told the media.

But Coach Jackson said the praise was all on the boys. "Me right now talking about it, I'm getting emotional," he said. "Because I've watched these boys grow. And they came a long way. They're amazing young men."

Alan Hardman, one of the rescued motorists, said it best: "I'll tell you what—I don't know how we would have done it without them," he said. "They didn't even hesitate."

True heroes never do.

ABOUT THE AUTHOR

JOANNE MATTERN is the author of many nonfiction books, including *War Dogs* and *Superhero Pets*. She and her family live in New York.